The Usborne
SECOND
Big Maze Book

Designed by
Ruth Russell and Nayera Everall

Illustrated by Mattia Cerato, Mark Ruffle,
Ruth Russell and Nayera Everall

Written by Phil Clarke

The mazes at the beginning of the book are easier
and they get more challenging as you go through.
You'll find solutions to all the mazes on pages 61-64.

Turtle tangle

Guide Hurtle the turtle through the winding weeds back to his mother.

Hurtle

Mother

2

All the animals

Every animal in the farm park is worth a look. Can you walk along every single path without going along one twice or crossing your own tracks?

ENTRANCE

WAY OUT

Sleds away

Find a clear route down the snowy mountainside to the finish line.
You can't go uphill.

START

FINISH

Skating search

Find the trail that will lead
Monty across the frozen lake
to his big sister.

Monty

Follow the herd

Help Andy the Alamosaurus find the way back to his herd. Stick to the paths and watch out for hungry green Tyrannosaurs.

Andy

Marina maze

It's time for some summer fun in the sand and sun. Guide the family from the boat to the beach, but don't disturb the fisherman.

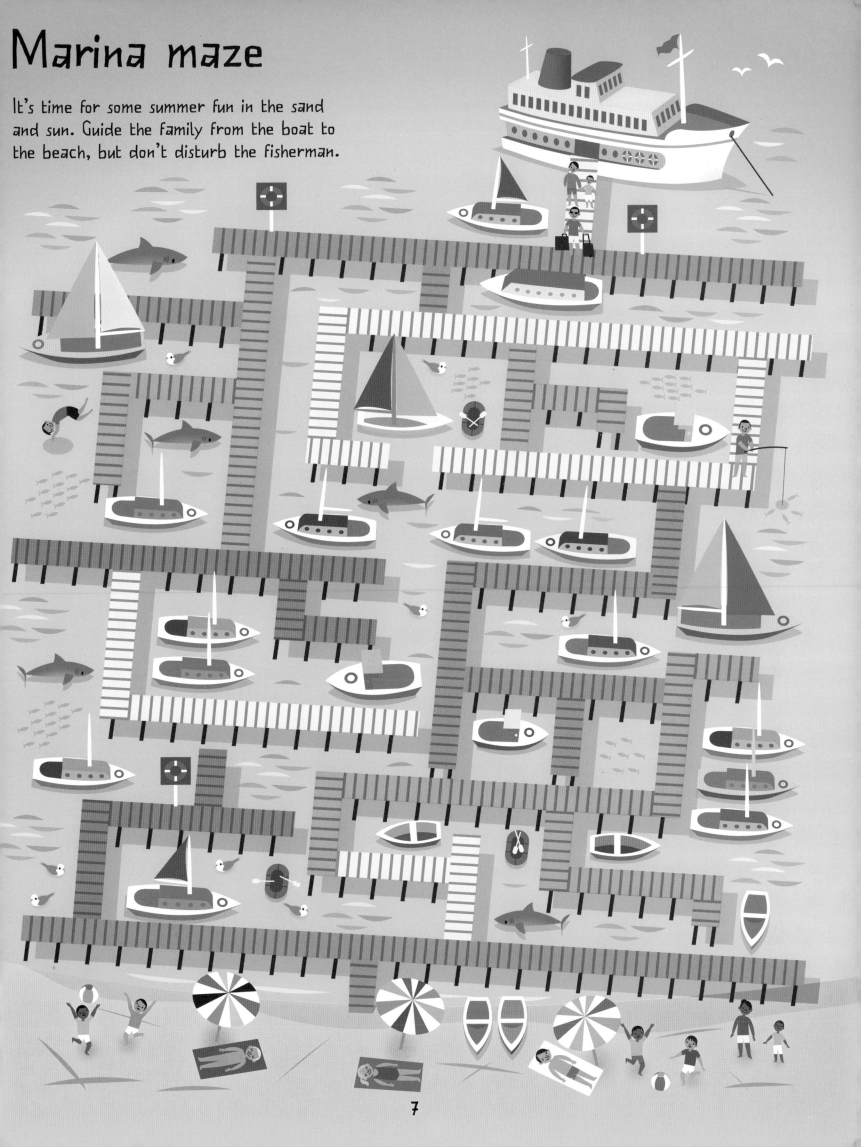

Graveyard getaway

You need to take a shortcut through the graveyard,
but some paths are blocked by zombies.
Can you make it in one piece?

Finish

Start

Too many tools

Frank has used every tool in his box to fix the car — and now he's feeling hungry. Guide him across his cluttered workshop to his lunchbox for a well-earned snack.

Start

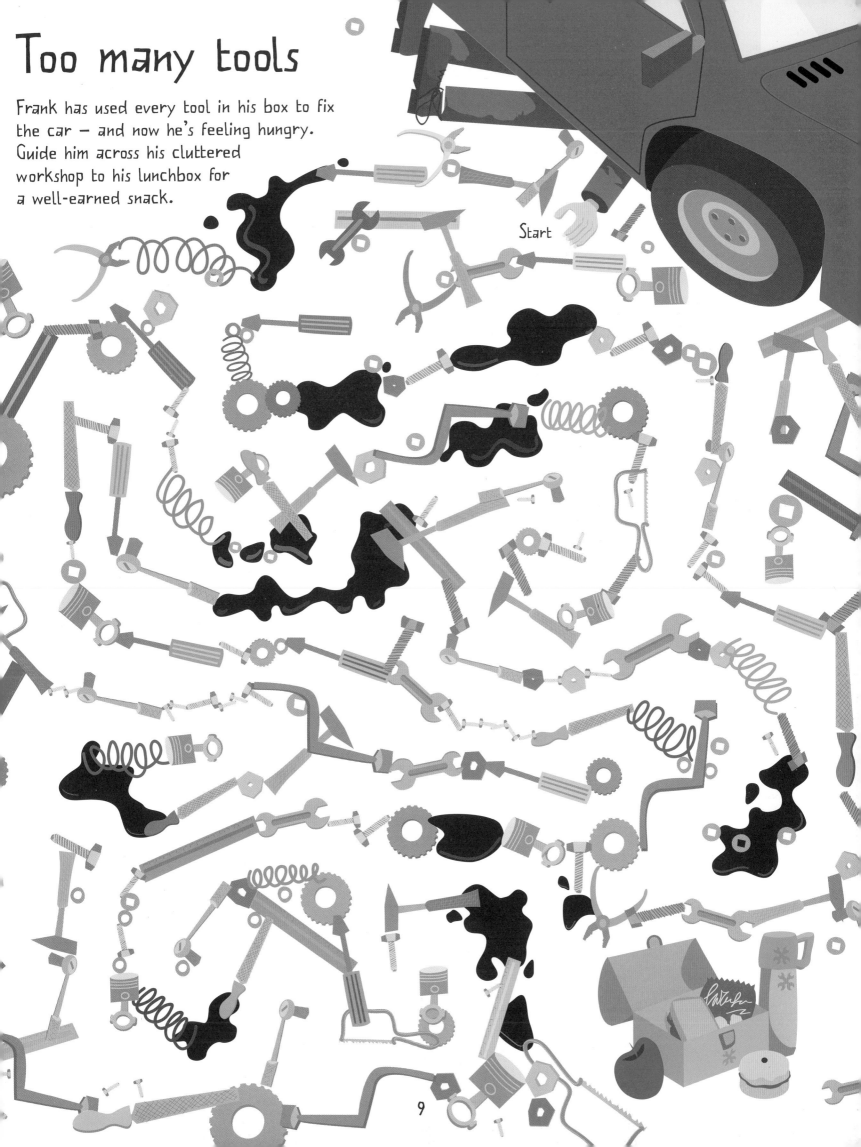

Busy beach

Vinny has bought ice creams for his parents — but the beach is very crowded and he's not sure where they are. Help him find them without stepping on anyone or anything, or getting his feet wet. His mother is wearing a pink hat and his father has yellow and green trunks.

Vinny

Fred's shed

Find your way through the allotments to Fred's shed. Keep to the paths and be careful not to step on any plants or garden tools.

Start here

Fred

Pecking hen

Help Hettie the hen to peck her way along
the trail of grain that leads to her house.

Hettie

Rooftop ramble

Camilla needs to get home in time for supper.
Help her find her way along the rooftops to
the only blue house in town. No jumping!

Camilla

Around the underground

Sam and Lucy want to go to the park. Find it on the map and plan their shortest possible route. They can only change to a different line at a circle stop.

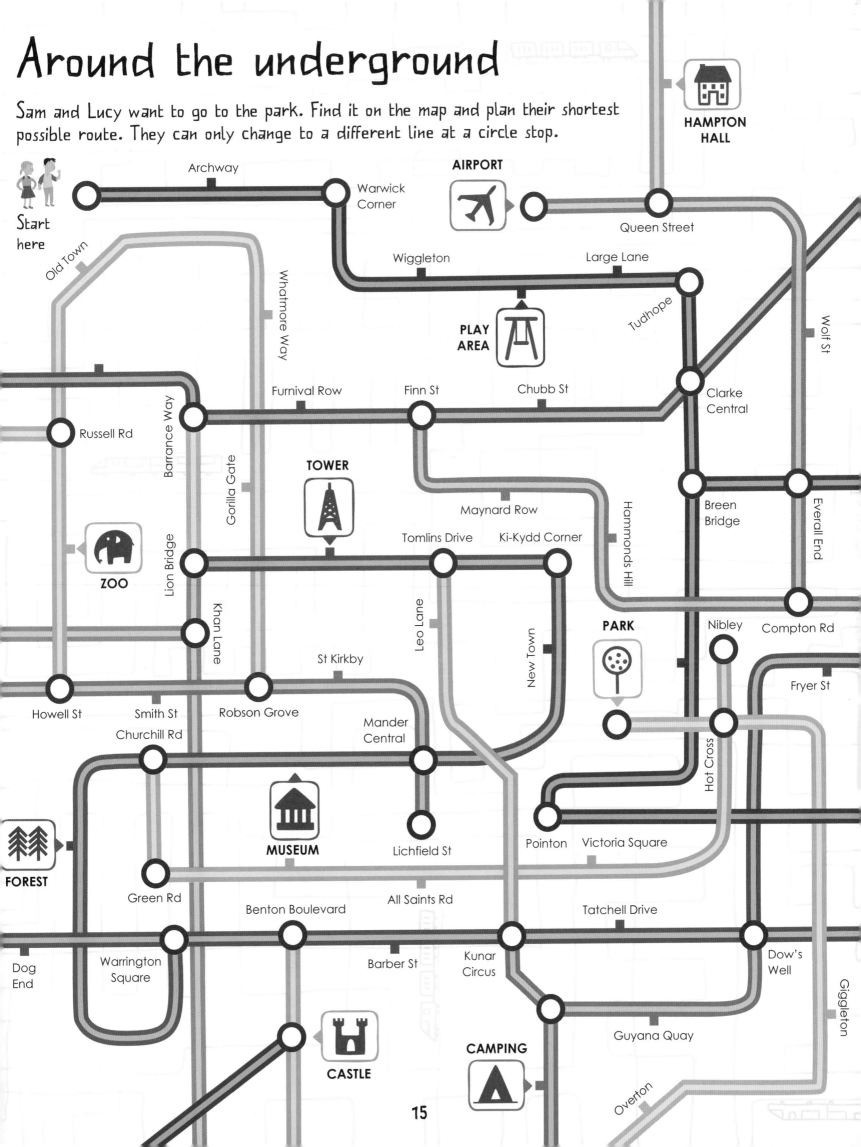

Start here

Old Town

Archway

Warwick Corner

AIRPORT

Queen Street

HAMPTON HALL

Wiggleton

Large Lane

Whatmore Way

PLAY AREA

Tudhope

Wolf St

Furnival Row

Finn St

Chubb St

Clarke Central

Russell Rd

Barrance Way

Gorilla Gate

TOWER

Maynard Row

Breen Bridge

Everall End

ZOO

Lion Bridge

Tomlins Drive

Ki-Kydd Corner

Hammonds Hill

PARK

Nibley

Compton Rd

Khan Lane

Leo Lane

New Town

Fryer St

St Kirkby

Howell St

Smith St

Robson Grove

Mander Central

Hot Cross

Churchill Rd

MUSEUM

Lichfield St

Pointon

Victoria Square

FOREST

Green Rd

Benton Boulevard

All Saints Rd

Tatchell Drive

Dog End

Warrington Square

Barber St

Kunar Circus

Dow's Well

Giggleton

Guyana Quay

CAMPING

CASTLE

Overton

15

Biking buddies

Josh is going to meet 12 friends on the
way to the park, but he mustn't use
the same road twice, or ride on the
grass. Which way should he go?

Josh

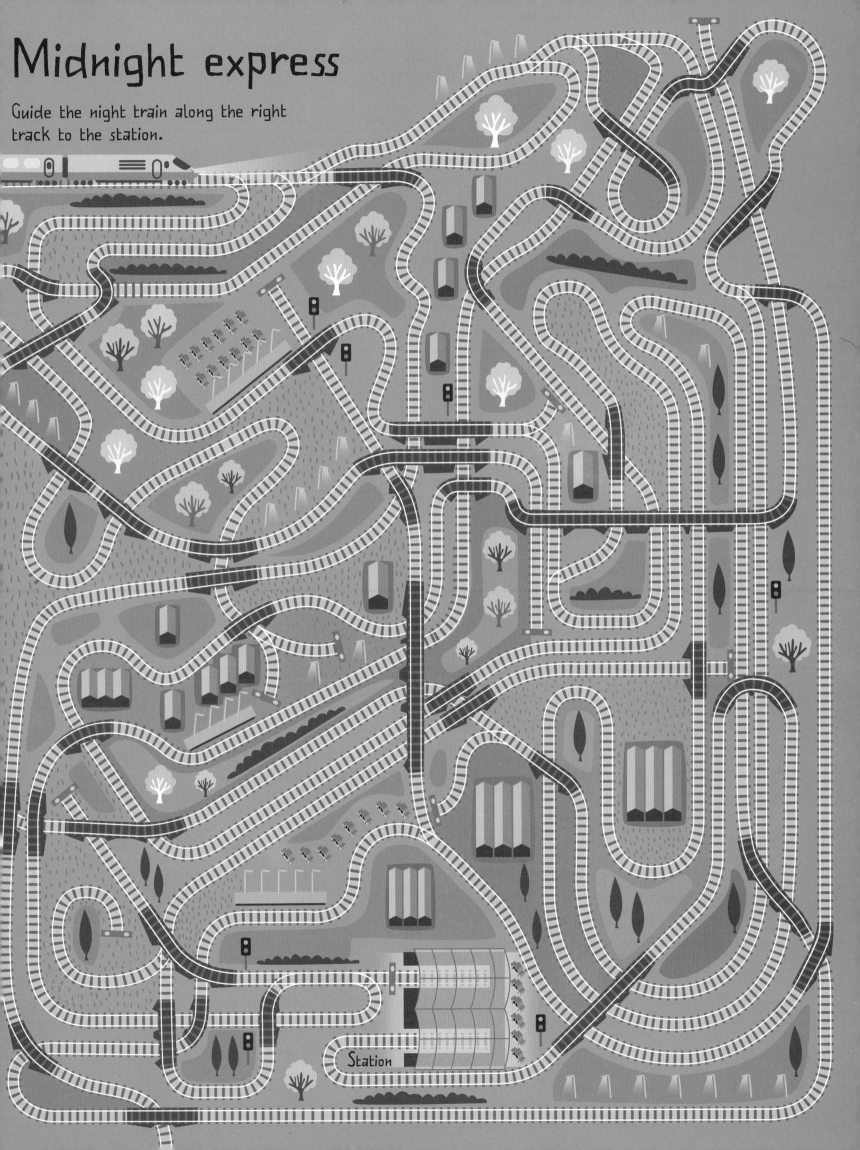

Midnight express

Guide the night train along the right track to the station.

Station

Loose screws

For a grabber to work, all the screws in its arm must be tight. Circle the only one that can pick up the treasure.

This screw is tight

This screw is loose

18

Easter eggs

Are you ready for an Easter egg hunt? Find the basket, gather all the eggs without going along the same route twice, then return to the start.

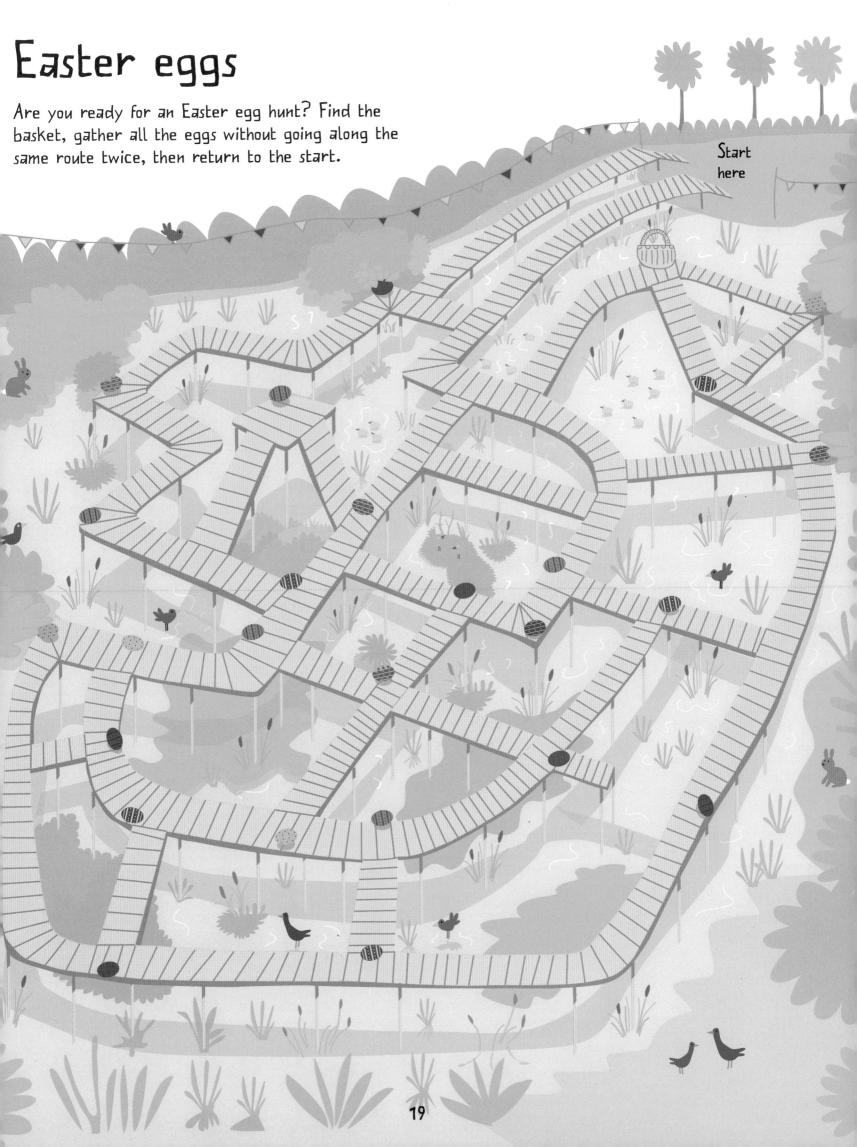

Start here

Treasure hunt

Guide Emily through the hedge maze to find
the treasure chest. To open each gate she'll
need to pick up its matching
key along the way.

Emily

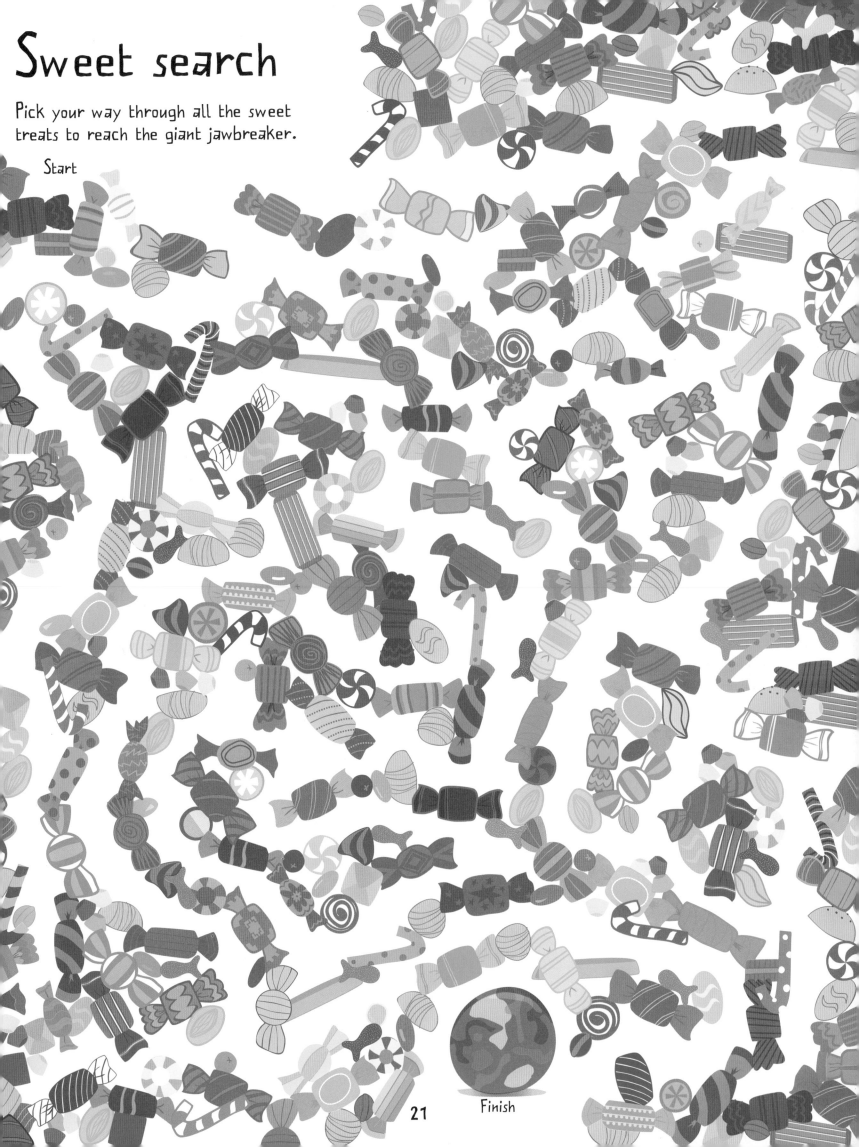

Sweet search

Pick your way through all the sweet treats to reach the giant jawbreaker.

Start

Finish

Damsel dash

Help the dashing prince reach the damsel in distress without passing any of the castle guards along the way.

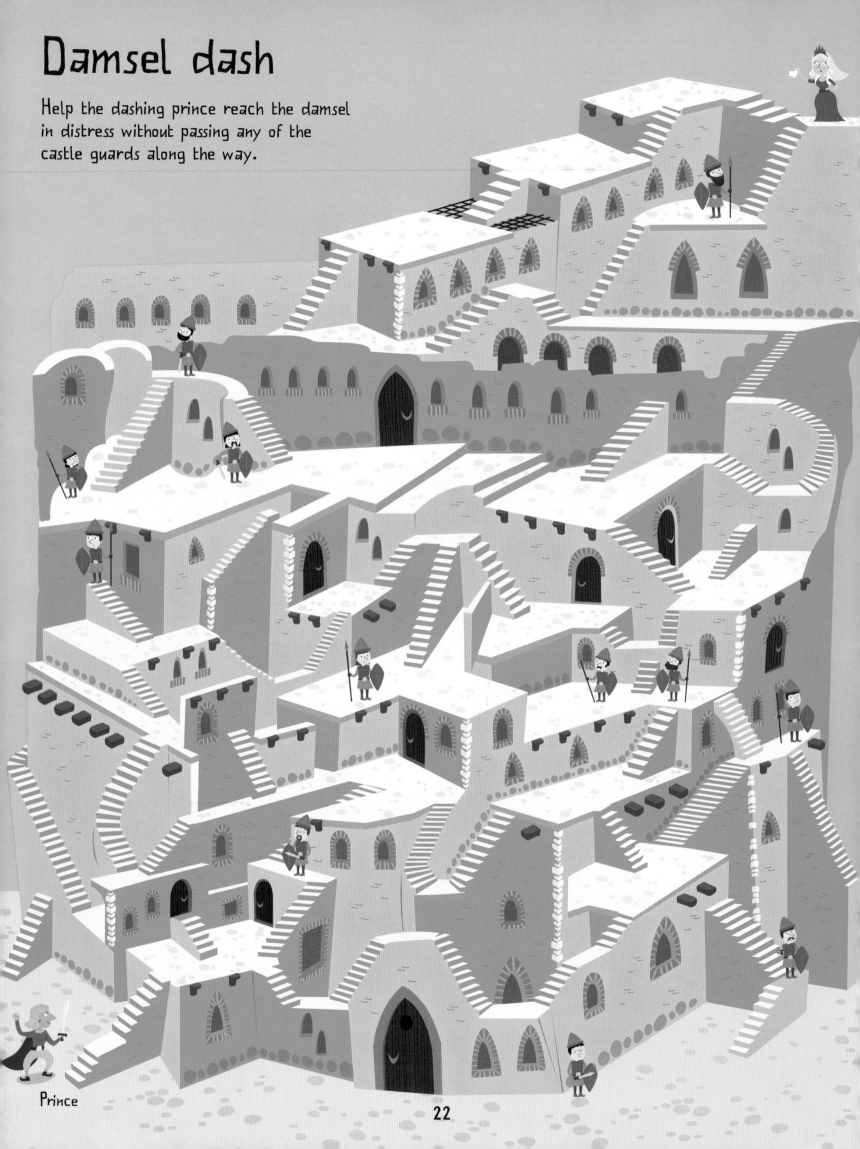

Prince

Hansel and Gretel

Hansel and Gretel know that they scattered exactly 30 white pebbles to lead them safely back to their father's cottage. Any more (or fewer) than this may take them to the wrong house. Help them find their way home.

Hansel and Gretel

Quail trail

Queenie the quail must reach her nest as quickly as she can — her eggs have started to hatch. She can't jump over rocks.

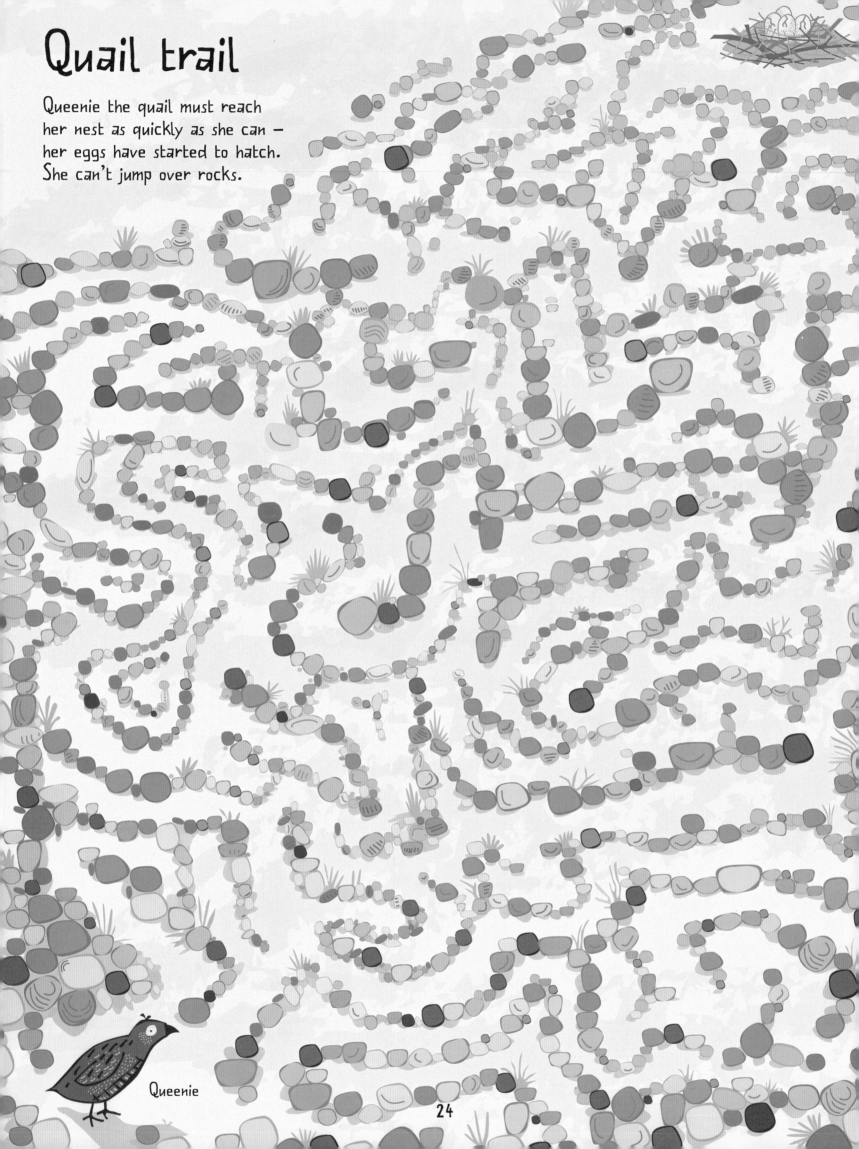

Queenie

Castle quest

Just one route will take the lost princess and her dog to the Castle of Snowy Canyon. Help her find her way before nightfall.

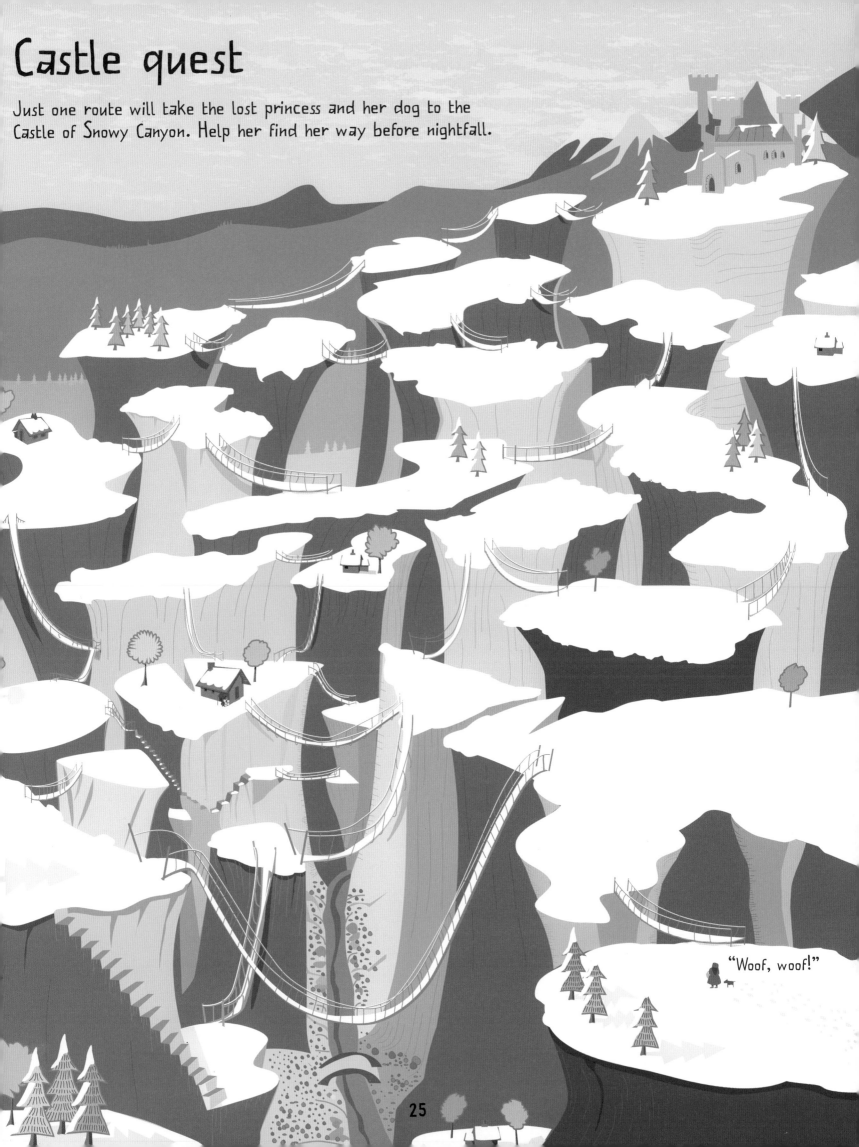

"Woof, woof!"

Around the airport

A plane is about to land at this bustling airport. Can you guide it safely to Terminal One? Some of the ways are busy or blocked, but there is one clear route for you to use.

TERMINAL 1

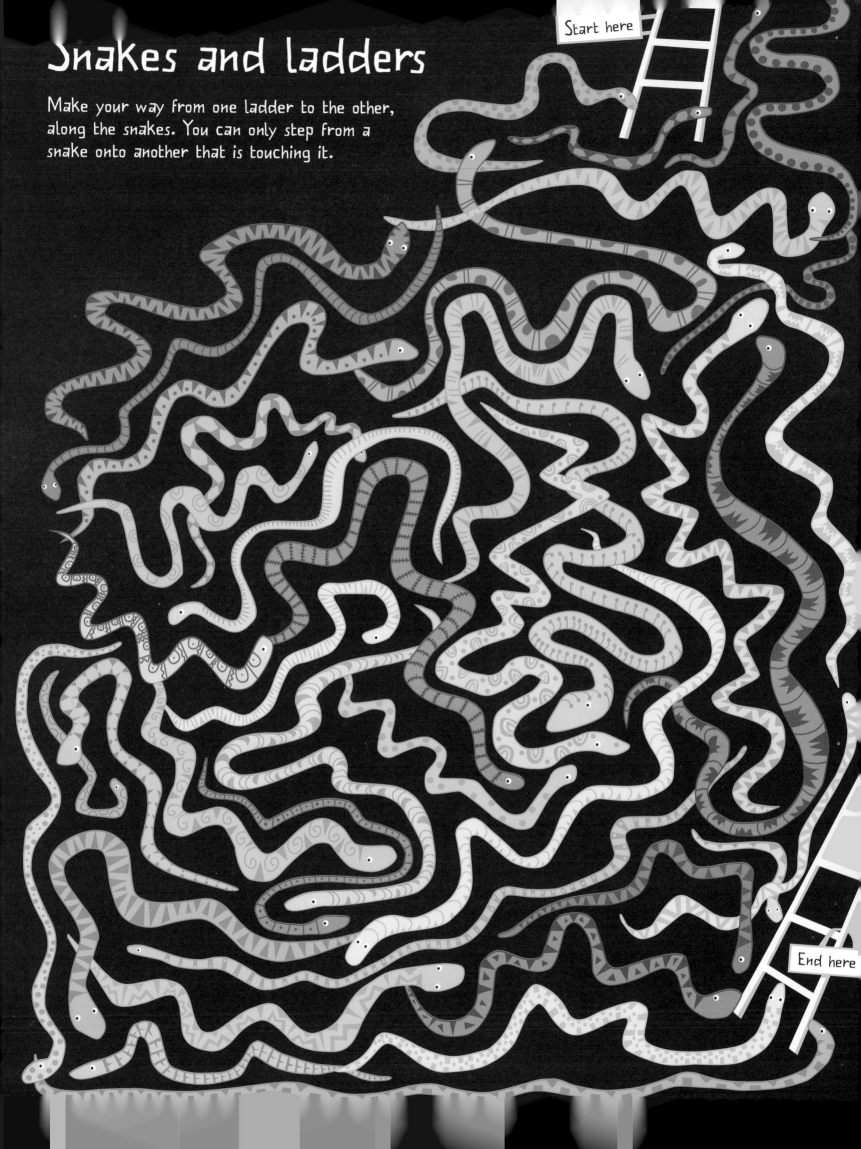

Snakes and ladders

Make your way from one ladder to the other, along the snakes. You can only step from a snake onto another that is touching it.

Start here

End here

Go, Billy goat!

It's feeding time in the meadow, but Billy the goat is at the top of the mountain. Can you help him find his way down?

Billy

At the racetrack

How can the red car win the race? Make sure you steer clear of obstacles and other cars.

Start

PIT STOP

30   Finish

Star search

Help Zorg the alien to return to his home planet.
He can travel on lines that go through stars,
but not through anything else.

Zorg

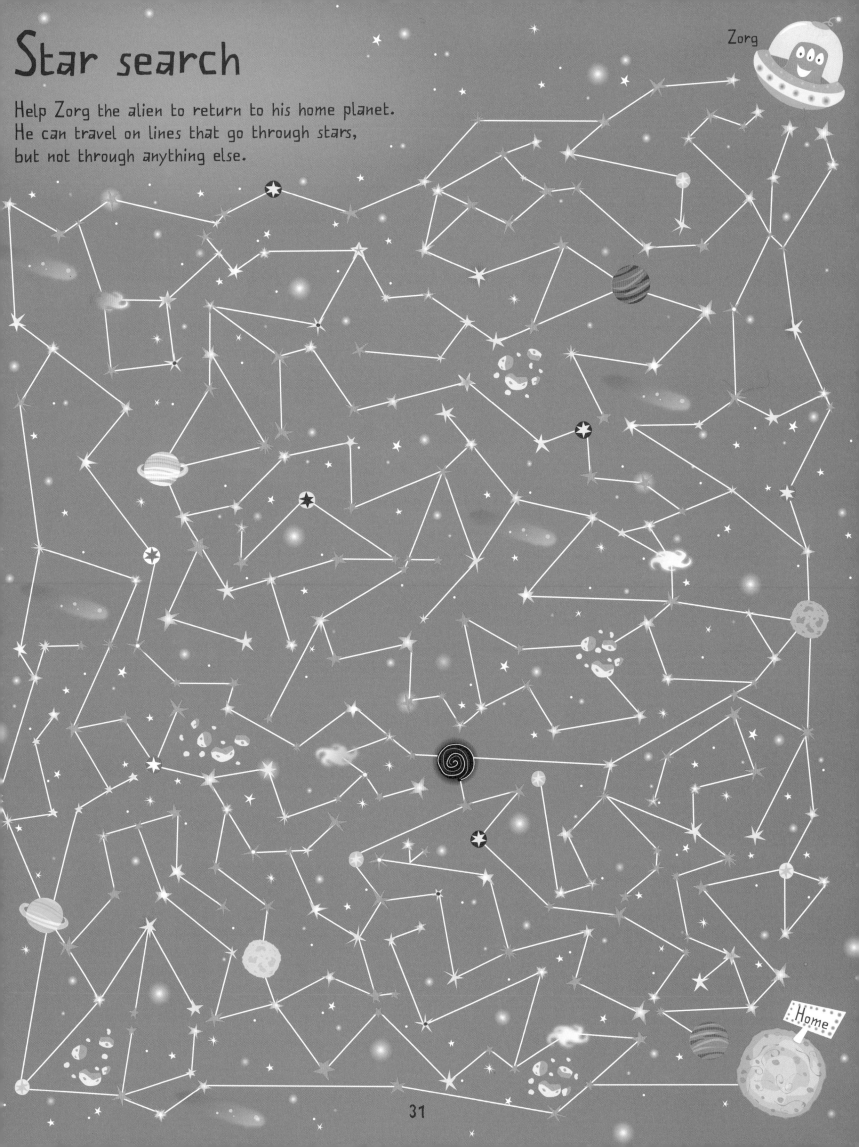

Home

Milkshake-maker

Find the route the strawberries must pass along to make it into the milkshake.

Toy inspectors

Only the toy with the highest score will make it out of the factory today. Follow the chutes to find out which it will be.

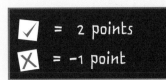

Feed the cows

Drive the red tractor between the fences, avoiding obstacles, to reach the hungry cows.

Hungry cows

Flight plan

Which way should Jessie fly to Mazeville?
She can only switch flight-paths at a
fuel stop, and needs the route with
the fewest stops along the way.

● = Fuel stop

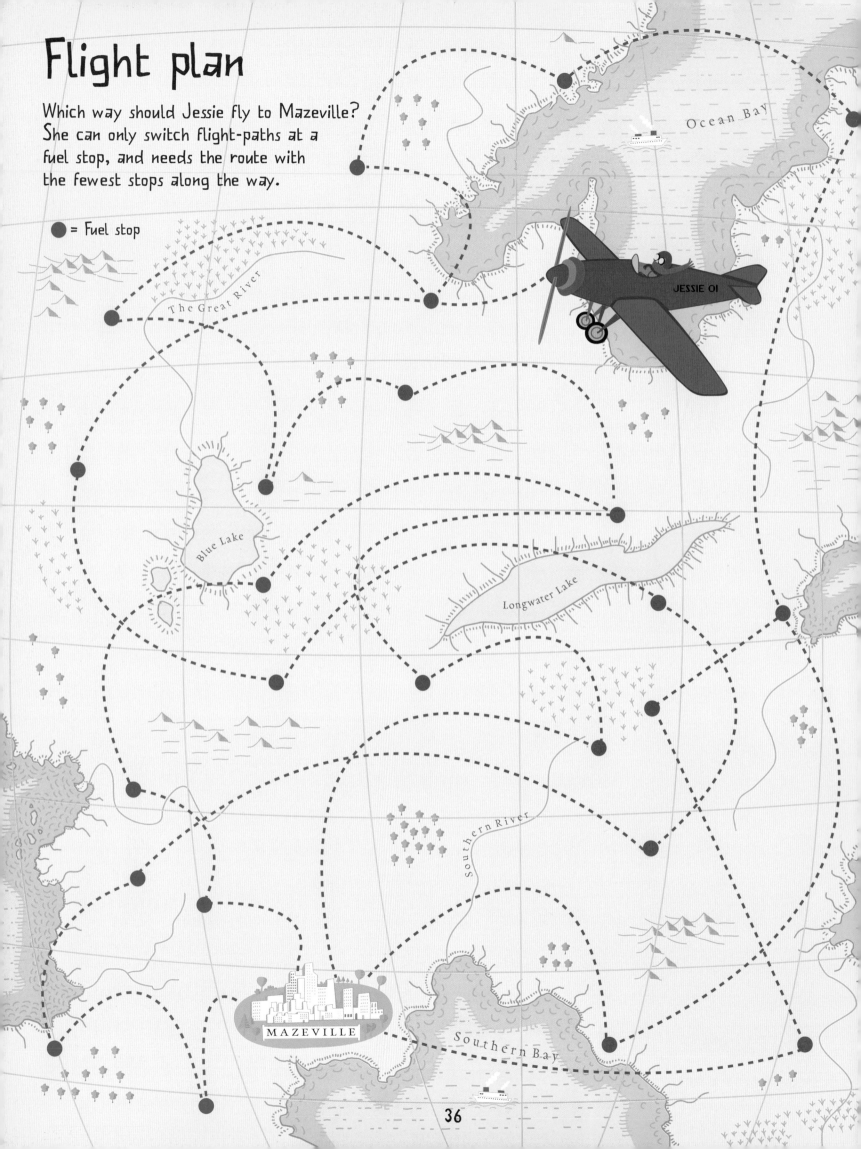

JESSIE 01

The Labyrinth

Find the route that leads the brave hero Theseus to the heart of the Labyrinth, where he hopes to defeat the fierce Minotaur who lurks there. Some passages are blocked by the remains of unlucky adventurers.

Theseus

Bear mountain

Hungry bears are prowling this mountain and it's starting to get dark. But a friendly crow has brought you some advice.

The black house is not safe. Leave it immediately and travel to the white castle as quickly as you can.

Zip, Zap, swap!

Zap wants to swap places with Zip. Each may only move diagonally, and only on squares of one shade. Zip's shade must be different from Zap's.

Fairground fun

Make the most of your day at the fair by planning a route visiting the Carousel, Ferris Wheel, Log Flume, Ghost House, Blast Off, Tornado Slide, Pirate Ship, Roller Coaster and Biggles Piggles, in that order. Visit the gift shop and grab a burger on the way out. Don't take the same path twice.

LOG FLUME
FEATURING THE 'DRENCH TRENCH'

Mr Munchies

GHOST HOUSE

BLAST OFF

FERRIS WHEEL

Roller COASTER 1

CAROUSEL

GIFT SHOP

BIGGLES PIGGLES

PIRATE SHIP

START FINISH

TORNADO SLIDE

Camel confusion

Guide the camels through the dunes to the desert market, without being bitten by scorpions.

Market

Eye in the sky

Help the helicopter pilot lead the fire truck along the quickest route to the burning house, while avoiding the tractors and other obstacles.

A walk in the park

Ellie is going to meet her friend at the fountain then visit each part of the park marked with a flag. Help her do it without walking through the same place twice or stepping on the grass. She needs to finish back at the park entrance.

Ellie

45

Hungry hamster

Henry the hamster is hungry. Help him find the food, without squeezing past the other hamsters.

Henry

Food

Treetop tea party

Help Doris the squirrel deliver her party invitations and return to the ground. She has to visit a friend in each treehouse, but can't use any section of a ladder more than once.

Start here

47

Mother and cub

Lead the mother polar bear back to her cub without crossing any of the cracks in the ice.

Cub

Mother

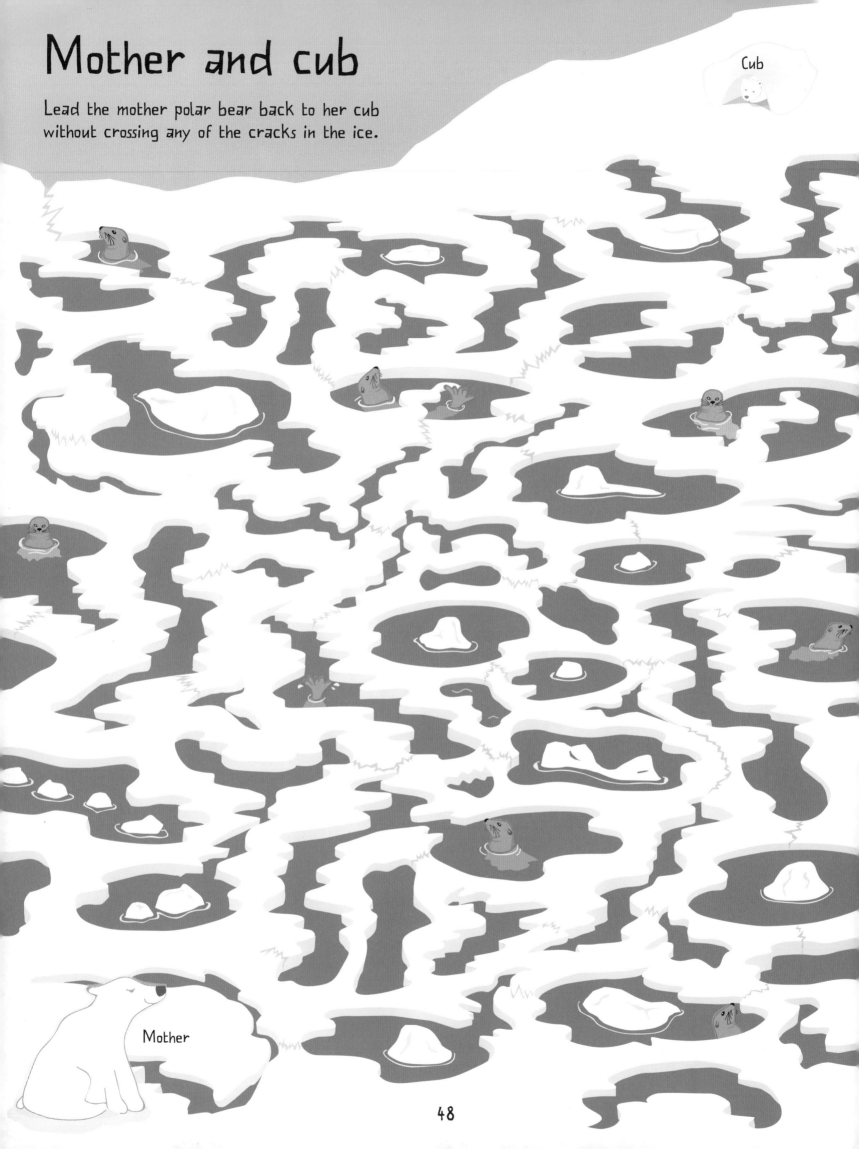

Suitcase search

Ben has lost his big, round, green suitcase. Can you spot it, and help him to weave his way through the stacks of cases to find it?

Ben

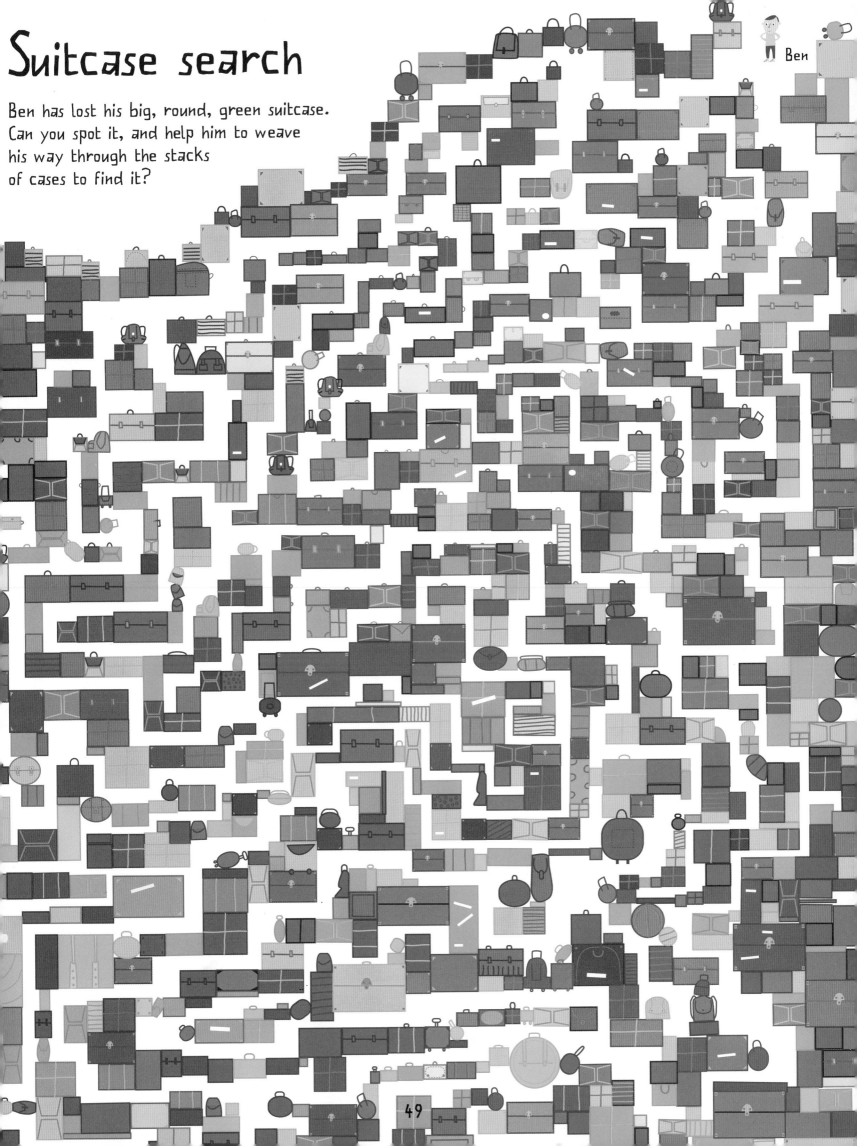

49

Resort route

The little red car is heading for the Seaside Beach Resort — but it's getting lost in all the tiny, twisty streets. Which way should it go?

Start here

SEASIDE
BEACH RESORT

50

Run, rabbit, run

Timmy the rabbit can only run along hedgerows — and he's too nervous to pass any fields with animals in them. He can run past gates, but only if they are closed. See if you can lead him to the woods.

Timmy

Woods

Snap-happy Sarah

Sarah wants to photograph all 16 domed buildings for her school project. Lead her to the front of each one, without taking any path more than once.

Sarah

Penguin in peril

Percy the penguin has left his surfboard back on the island. Guide him there safely between the waves, avoiding sharks, and other penguins.

Percy

Market day

Carefully choose the route that lets you pick up all the shopping on the list in the right order. You shouldn't take any path twice, and remember to finish with an ice cream.

1 Pair of boots
2 Apples
3 Cheese
4 Flowers
5 Bread
6 Balloon
7 Umbrella
8 Eggs
9 Kite
10 Fish
11 Ice cream

Start here

ices

BOOTS

Cheese
Fruit & Veg

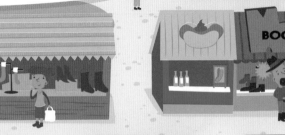

Flowers

FISH

BLOOMS

BAKERY

BREAD

BALLOONS

Balloons

Umbrellas

Kites

Farm Eggs

BOOKS
GIFTS

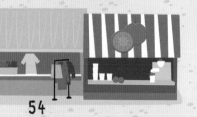
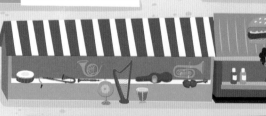
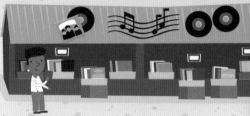

Desert gold

Which underground passage will
lead you to the treasure chamber?

Start here

Art gallery

Your ticket for the art gallery lets you visit every room just once.
Plan a route that allows you to see every exhibit before you leave.

Volcano countdown

Quick! Escape the bubbling volcano before it erupts. The only safe place is the palm tree island. Watch out for sea serpents...

Parking puzzle

Find the nearest parking space for each car waiting at the entrance.
Drivers may only park between two cars of the same style as their own.
They can drive through empty parking spaces, but
only between cars of exactly the same shade as
theirs. And don't forget it's a one-way system!

ENTRANCE

58

Testing tubes

This experiment is getting a little out of control. Assist the scientist by finding the correct route from the flask of green liquid, along the glass tubing, to the bubbling water tank.

Start

Finish

2. Turtle tangle

3. All the animals

4. Sleds away

5. Skating search

6. Follow the herd

7. Marina maze

8. Graveyard getaway

9. Too many tools

10-11. Busy beach

12. Fred's shed

13. Pecking hen

14. Rooftop ramble

15. Around the underground

16. Biking buddies

17. Midnight express

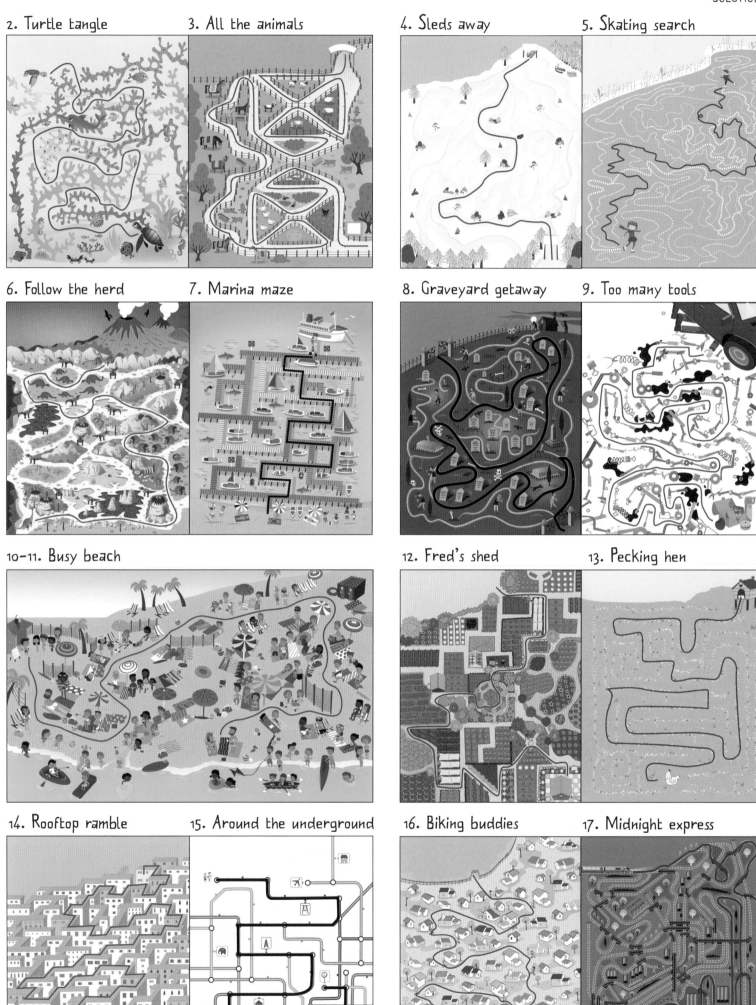

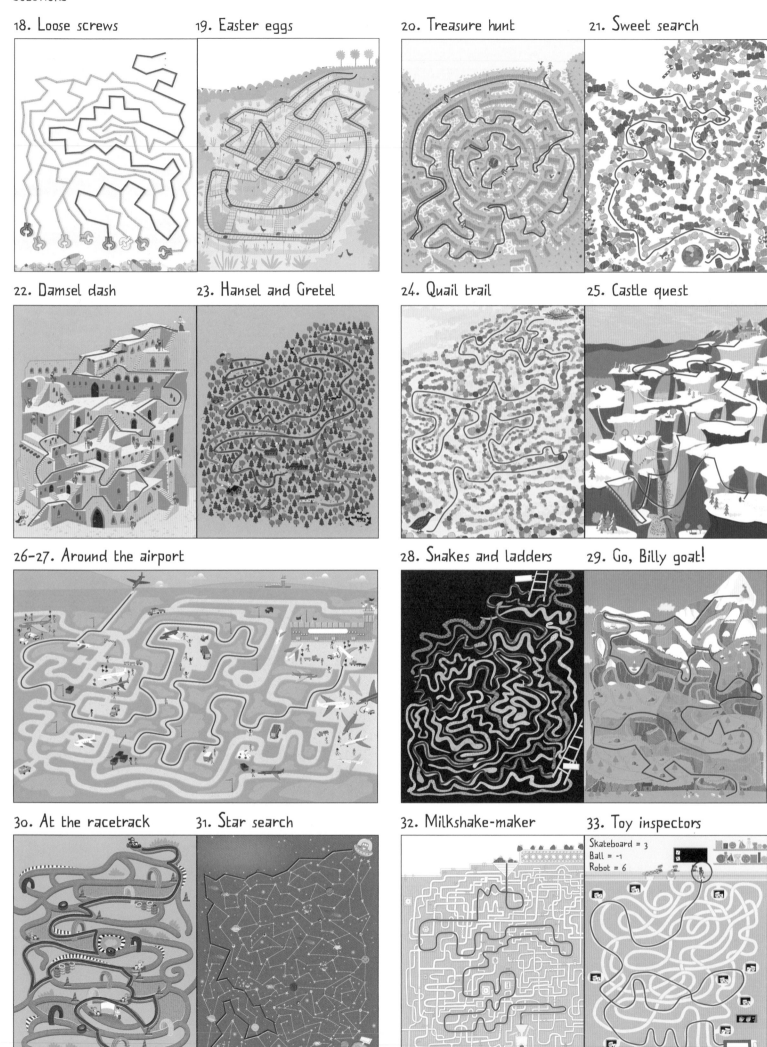

18. Loose screws

19. Easter eggs

20. Treasure hunt

21. Sweet search

22. Damsel dash

23. Hansel and Gretel

24. Quail trail

25. Castle quest

26-27. Around the airport

28. Snakes and ladders

29. Go, Billy goat!

30. At the racetrack

31. Star search

32. Milkshake-maker

33. Toy inspectors

Skateboard = 3
Ball = -1
Robot = 6

34-35. Feed the cows

36. Flight plan

37. The Labyrinth

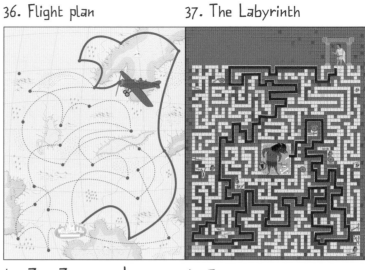

38-39. Bear mountain

40. Zip, Zap, swap!

41. Fairground fun

42. Camel confusion

43. Eye in the sky

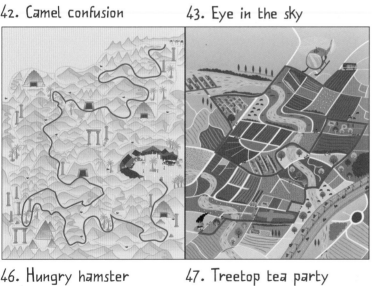

44-45. A walk in the park

46. Hungry hamster

47. Treetop tea party

48. Mother and cub

49. Suitcase search

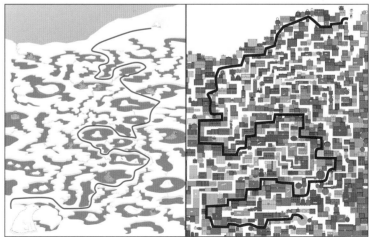

50. Resort route

51. Run, rabbit, run

52. Snap-happy Sarah

53. Penguin in peril

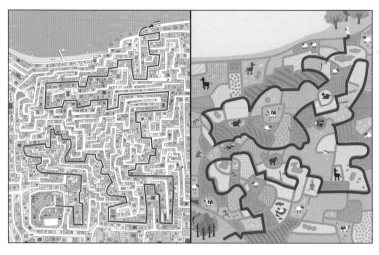

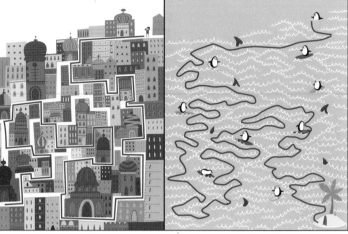

54. Market day

55. Desert gold

56. Art gallery

57. Volcano countdown

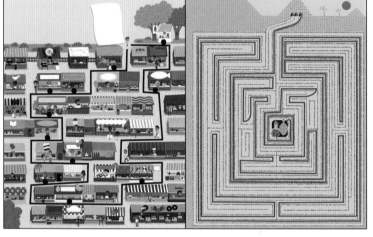
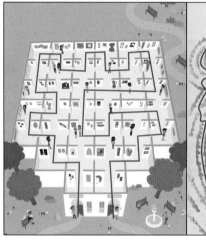

58–59. Parking puzzle

60. Testing tubes

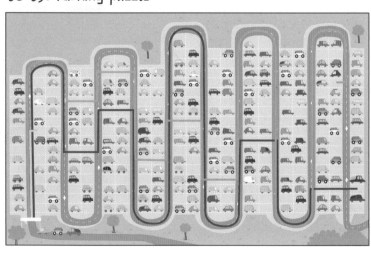
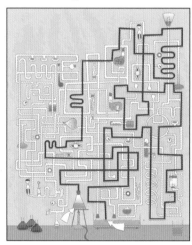

Acknowledgements

Additional designs by Tim Ki-Kydd

Cover design by Candice Whatmore

Edited by Sam Taplin and Kirsteen Robson

With thanks to our maze testers: Janey Harold and Faye Jones